Adventures in Patchwork

Adventures in Patchwork

Dorothea Nield

Mills & Boon Limited, London

First published in Great Britain 1975 by Mills & Boon
Limited, 17–19 Foley Street, London W1A 1DR.

ISBN 0 263.05591.4

Made and printed in Great Britain by
T. & A. Constable Ltd.
Hopetoun Street
Edinburgh

Contents

Acknowledgements

I am sincerely grateful to the following:

Embroidery, published by the Embroiderers' Guild, in which my use of isometric paper for pattern drafting first appeared (Volume XXIII No. 2, 1972);

Muriel Root for kindly allowing her patchwork panel on page 53 to be photographed;

Margaret Taylor for her design on page 56;

Margaret Swain for her help in compiling the list of places where patchwork can be seen;

and also Evelyn Longard.

Introduction

Many patchworkers have explored the designs based on hexagons, and with the use of plain and patterned fabrics have achieved interesting variations. There are, however, many more shapes that can be used to produce individual designs, and with care the effect from more unusual fabrics can be used. This book is intended as a guide to plan patterns and designs with practical directions in the interpretation. Thus, it is hoped the worker will gain greater pleasure from patchwork in all its variations.

The layout of the book is arranged in the form of lessons so that while the relative newcomer to patchwork can benefit from the first lessons, the more experienced worker can choose to move ahead.

Patterns are of vital importance, but an understanding of colour effects and tonal values is necessary and therefore included. Three lessons demonstrate how an idea can be developed into practical patchwork.

Boxes based on patchwork shapes, an unusual method from a Spanish skirt, also the unique pattern of the Seminole Indians are included to encourage the worker to search for an individual style and interpretation in her patchwork.

Making and Joining Hexagon Patches

Patchwork is a method by which pieces of material are joined together to make a whole design and a complete area of fabric. First learn the technique before advancing to personal design. A hexagon shape (six-sided) is the easiest to handle, so buy a 1½" equilateral hexagon metal template, and a matching plastic window template. The metal one is to cut firm paper shapes accurately, and the plastic window shows the position of the pattern of the fabric in relation to the hexagon outline. As the plastic window template is slightly larger than its metal companion, it is used for cutting out the fabric patches, and when the material is cut against the edge, there will be a turning allowance of the correct size to fold over the paper shape. The turnings are tacked to the paper and the resultant patches are then stitched together. This is briefly the basic method. More detailed instructions are given on the following pages.

Materials The ideal material is a cotton of poplin weight. Avoid any heavily treated, crease-resistant materials, sailcloth or glazed cotton, as these are more difficult to fold and stitch, and the glazed surface marks permanently if a wrong stitch is unpicked. To build up a pattern, choose floral, striped or varied designs with at least one matching plain colour. If the article to be made needs to be washable, choose fast-dyed materials.

Thread Fine sewing cotton; white for the light colours and black for the dark shades. The usual size is No. 50 or No. 80, but it should be adjusted to the weight of the material to give a firm, yet not bulky stitch.

Thimble The use of a thimble is recommended as it enables the worker to concentrate on the rhythm of the stitching, rather than on the movement of pushing the needle.

Needles As for all sewing, choose a needle that takes the thread without wear, yet is fine enough to stitch easily through the material. Sizes 9 or 10 will be right for general use. Whether it is a sewing, crewel or between needle is the personal preference of the worker.

Paper to cut the shapes As a guide choose the thickness of note-paper. Scrap paper can be used, but it must all be of a similar thickness to prevent any variation in the size of the patches, and any print should not mark the fabric.

With the metal template, mark on the paper and cut accurately.

Using the window template, move it over the pattern of the material to find the most attractive or interesting arrangement within the shape, then cut round the edges of the template. Some workers prefer to pencil round the template before cutting, which is quite satisfactory—but do not use a soft pencil, such as B, as it will make the material dirty. H or HB is the pencil to use on light colours, and a white pencil on dark colours.

The question always arises as to the position of the shape in relation to the warp and weft threads of the material. On plain colours it is a good rule to keep the direction of the threads the same throughout the piece of work. This will prevent too much 'play' and enable the finished work to lie flat. On patterned fabrics the arrangement of the design is always the most important consideration.

Metal template and window template in position on patterned fabric. (Photo-graph: Paul Meidman)

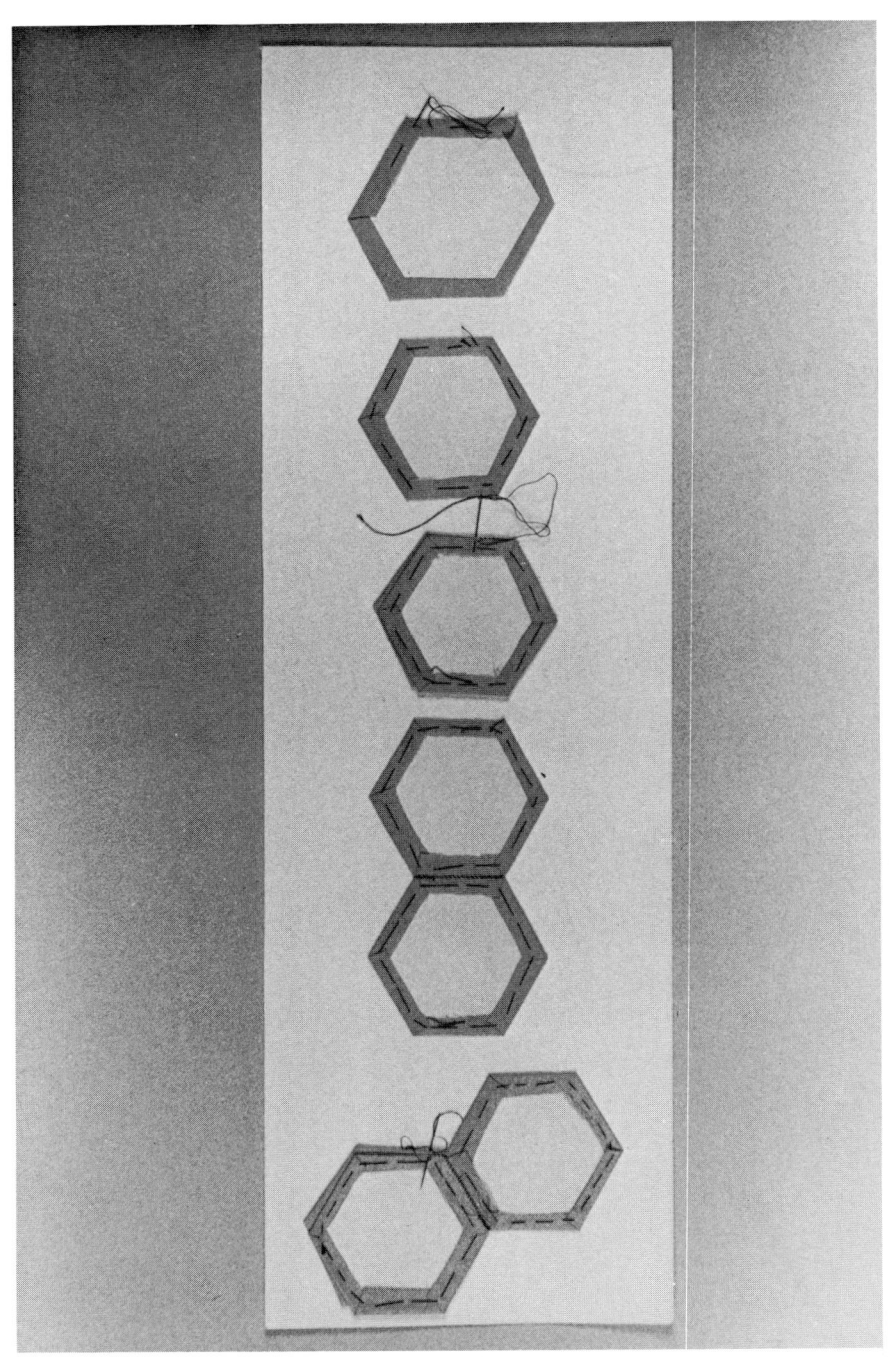

Stages of folding, tacking and stitching hexagon patches. (Photograph: Paul Meidman)

Hold or pin the paper template in the centre on the wrong side of the material patch. Fold over each edge and tack. With practice the size of the tacking stitch can be adjusted so that the corner folds are held in place by putting the needle down into the fold. Avoid using a knot and back stitches as this will save considerable time when removing the tacking stitches at the end, before making up the article. It is sufficient to allow a short end of thread at both ends of the tacking.

There are two schools of thought on tacking right through the turnings, paper and patch. One is that only the turnings and paper should be tacked. To achieve this, hold the needle rather flat, avoiding a stabbing position. This method is necessary when the needle leaves a mark on the fabric, such as on glazed surfaces.

However, tacking through to the right side (through all turnings) has the advantage of being quicker and will also ensure complete control of any material that is difficult to handle.

To join, hold two patches right sides together, and with sewing thread oversew the two edges together, working from right to left. In this position the first finger and thumb of the left hand can grip the patches and guide them evenly towards the over-sewing. Only pick up a small stitch on the fold, so that the paper templates are not caught up in the sewing.

To commence a new thread, lay the end of the cotton where it will be oversewn by the first three or four stitches.

To finish off a thread oversew back three or four stitches, crossing over the previous stitches.

When oversewing, the best results are obtained by keeping the needle at right angles (straight across) to the edge. This gives the smallest stitch on the right side.

Having joined two patches together on one side, the next hexagon is stitched in position. The same needleful of thread can follow on to the other patches, thus avoiding too many beginnings and endings.

There is often a tendency to slacken the tension of the oversewing when manipulating the corners with a new patch. This will result in larger stitches showing on the right side. To avoid this, there should be a conscious tightening of the thread until the correct tension becomes natural.

When the patchwork is complete, press lightly on the right side and remove the tacking, which will release the paper templates. It is now ready for making-up.

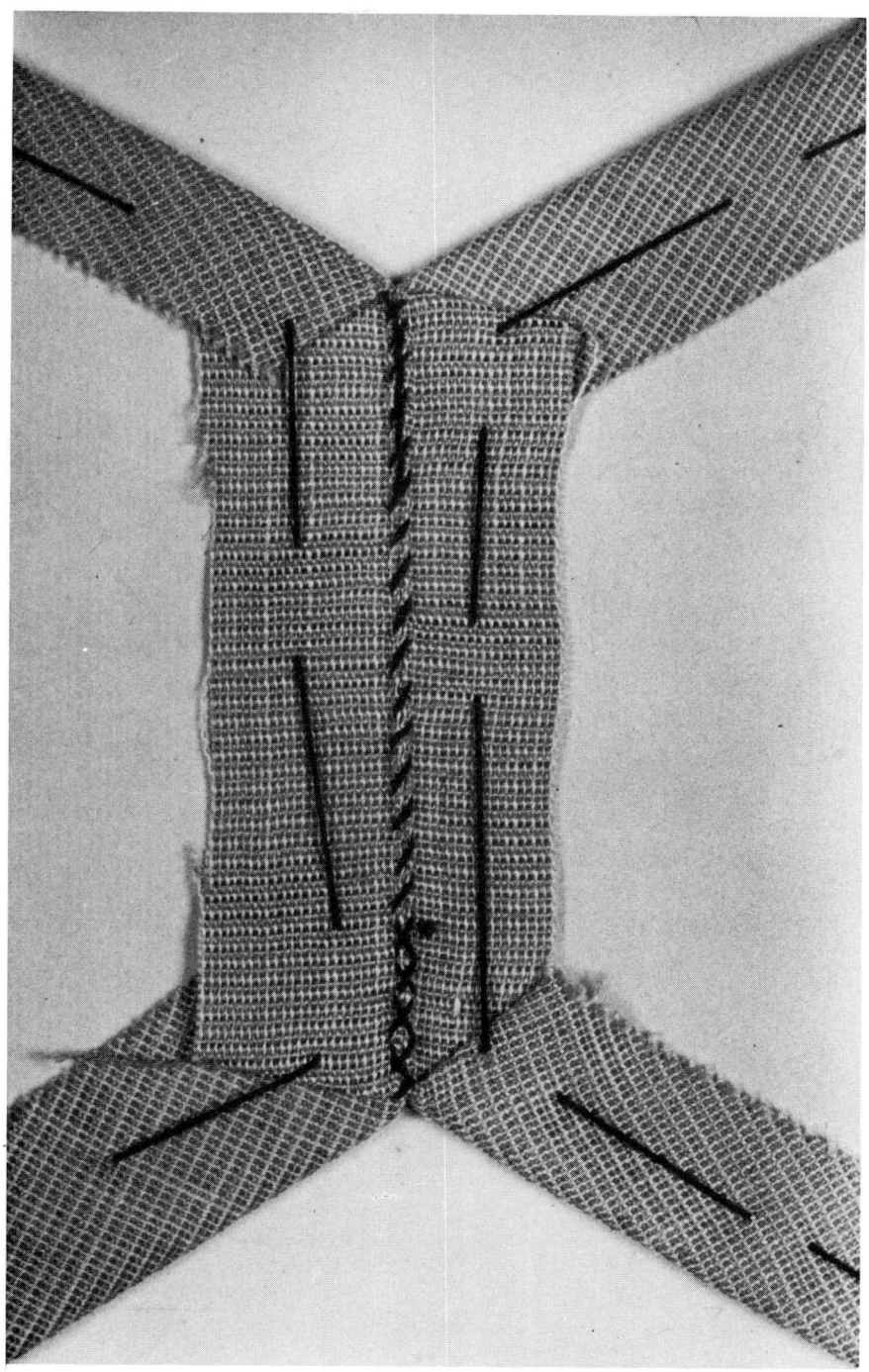

Enlargement of the join between two hexagon patches. (Photograph: Paul Meidman)

ROSETTE MOTIF

The conventional rosette motif is a simple arrangement of seven hex–agons, one being central and usually of a contrasting colour or tone (see the photograph opposite).

An alternative arrangement of this motif was devised because, as often happens with patchwork, the worker likes to make the motifs when travelling or on holiday and at a later date join the motifs to form the whole article. In the case of large articles, such as a bedspread, the work soon becomes bulky to handle. By planning a larger motif more work can be done before the final joining.

Five central hexagons are stitched in a straight line and the shape built up around these. As can be seen in the illustration on page 19, the second row is floral, with the centre and third rows linking the colours. Round these three rows a grey and white fine checked material forms a frame and it is used round each motif.

Finally, the linking of the motifs is made by a single line of navy and green smudgy–patterned material.

To level the edges, half-patterns are worked at each end, and a simple border using navy, check and bril– liant plain colours forms the side borders.

Various arrangements of the conventional rosette motif using seven hexagonal patches. (Photograph: Paul Meidman)

For this bedspread, a $1\frac{3}{8}''$ template was used, and a single three–foot bed required nineteen motifs and four half–motifs.

Bedspread . . .

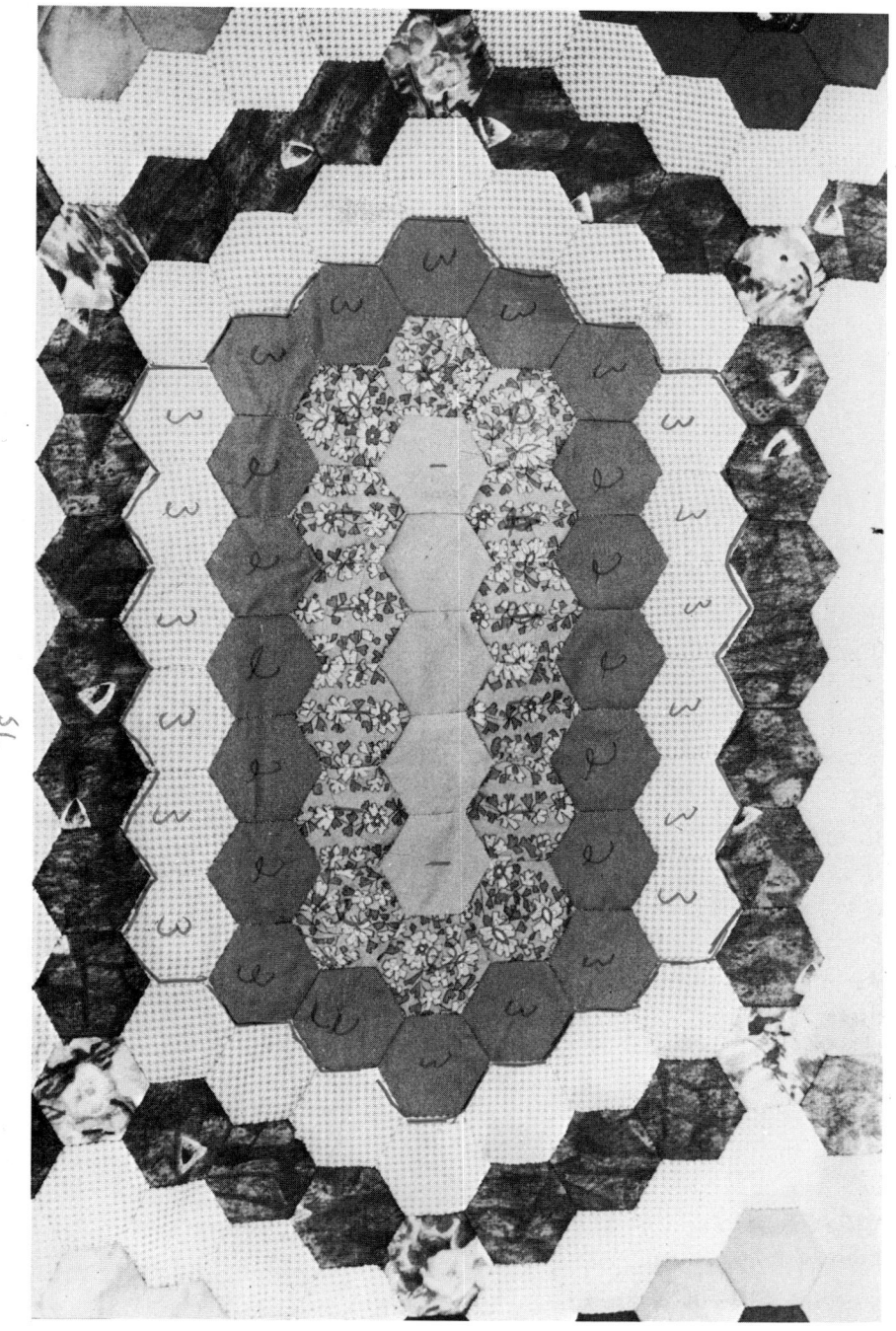

and close-up of one of the motifs. (*Photographs: Paul Meidman*)

Making and Joining Diamond Patches

There are two diamond templates available:

(a) those with angles of 60° and 120°, which are used to form a six–pointed star and will fit in with hexagons

(b) those known as long diamond with angles of 50° and 130°, which are used to form an eight–pointed star.

Cut the patches as explained for hexagons, then begin the tacking at the flatter point and fold towards the sharp point. The recognised method is to fold to the top, turn over across the point so that the short fold rests to the left of the point. Then continue making the turning on the next side, holding the point by firm tacking.

An alternative method, which is preferred by some workers, is to fold to the top, then down the other side, leaving the extra turnings flapping at the point. The advantage of this method is that when the patches are stitched together, any slight variation due to small differences in fabric can be easily adjusted.

In some parts of a box design, six points meet which can be difficult to manipulate, causing a small gap. To avoid this make sure two opposite patches meet, and the others can then be fitted in.

The two diamond templates. (Photograph: Paul Meidman)

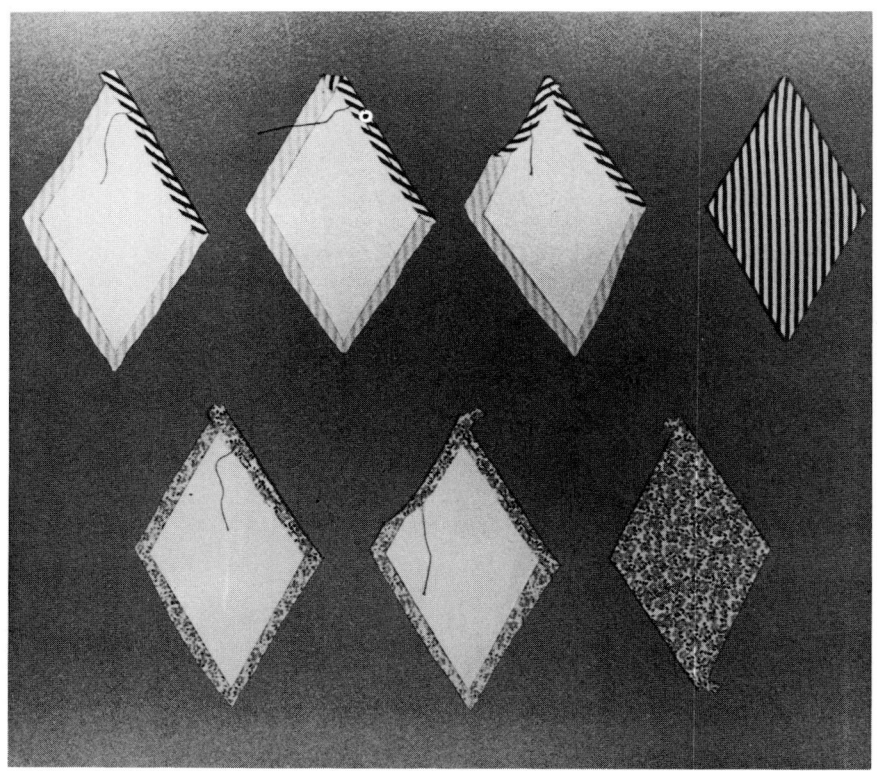

Two methods of folding and tacking a diamond patch. (Photograph: Paul Meidman)

Box Patterns

Hexagons, if divided into three equal parts, form diamonds which can give a box effect. The most satisfactory way to achieve this is to choose fabrics which give a light, medium and dark side to each box.

Plain or striped colours are useful, though a floral pattern that relates in shape and size to the patch will give a completely different effect, particularly if it is used on the light side only.

The patches are joined together with the light and dark patches in the same position throughout. This will give the effect of a light shining on one side.

An experiment with this idea was carried out by using white, grey and black, then in two areas of the design all–white patches formed the box shapes. In a strange way there is an illusion that the boxes continue. This idea could be explored further, perhaps using areas of patterned patches, or variations of colour or tone, always making sure that the box effect is not lost.

It was found necessary at this stage of designing patchwork to plan the ideas on paper first, so a printed paper called 'Isometric' was used (see page 84). On this hexagons, diamonds and triangles can be drawn in various sizes, guided by the printed lines.

An experimental arrangement of the box pattern

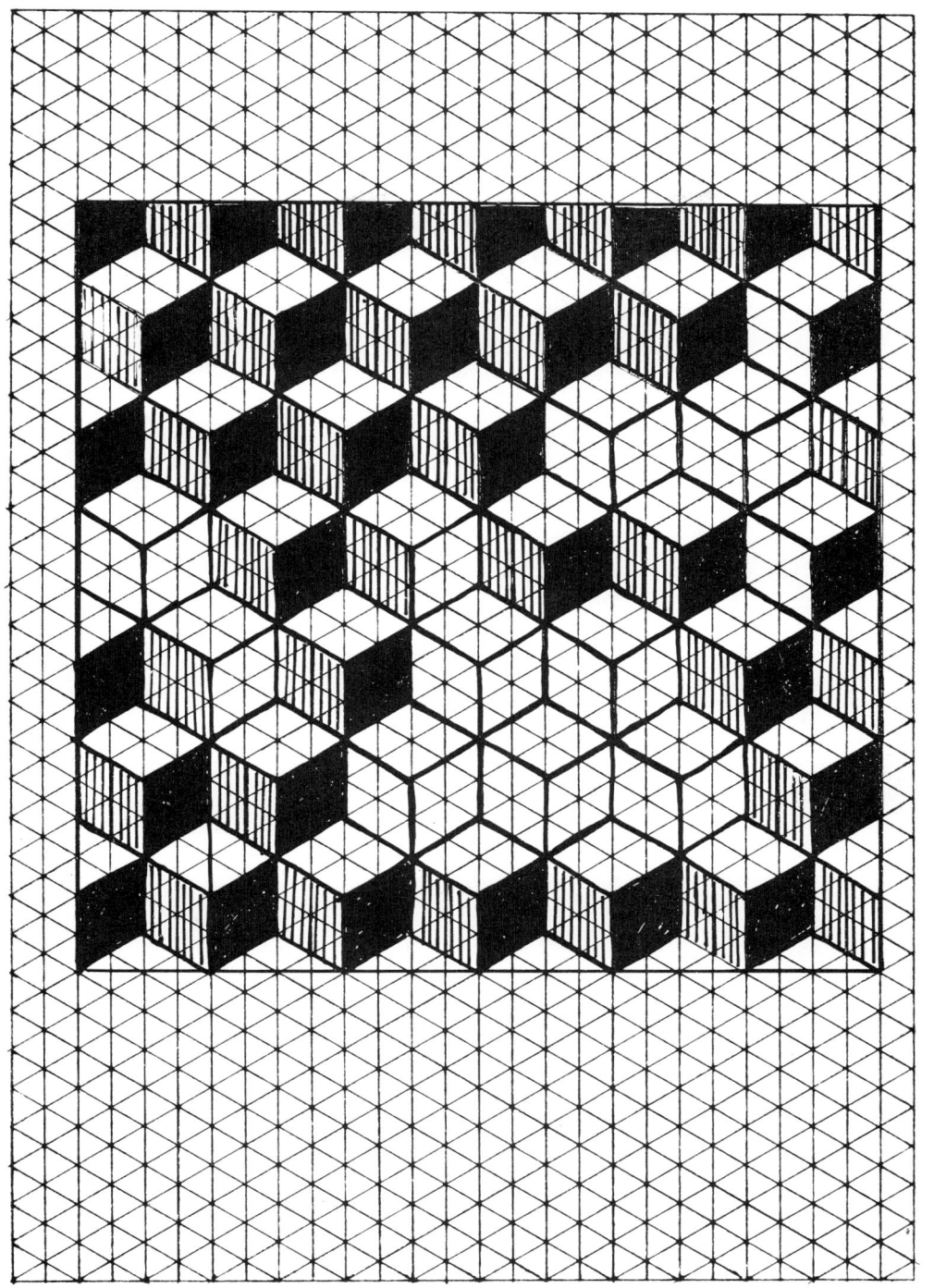

Diamond Patterns

Diamonds can be arranged to form all–over patterns and borders.

First outline the shapes, then using colour or tone develop the effect. The use of light, medium and dark shading in pencil saves the scheme from becoming too complicated. Some of the most effective patchwork is created by great tonal contrast between light and dark.

To translate the sketched design into fabrics first, ignoring the colours, arrange the fabrics into the three categories of light, medium and dark, then explore the combination of three colours, one from each group, e.g. dark purple, medium green and white.

This method can be used to develop fresh thoughts on colour and is particularly useful for workers who lack confidence when handling colour. If in doubt, make up small areas of the patches and compare the final effect. Sometimes viewing the results through a mirror or pinned on to a wall will help to decide the best arrangement.

Another Way to Plan a Colour Scheme

On isometric paper outline several repeats of the shapes designed for making into patchwork. Then various schemes can be coloured in, using paint, coloured pencils or perhaps coloured paper.

A useful simplification that can often ensure a satisfactory scheme is to plan within certain limitations, e.g. blue and green, red and pink, brown and yellow; in other words the colours that are near each other in the colour spectrum.

The next stage in exploring colour is to introduce one sharp, contrasting colour only. The quantity of this is important. Commence with a little, then try more. There will come a stage when too much will swamp the rest of the colours and the whole design will become unbalanced. If each try-out is coloured separately, it is easier to compare and choose the most satisfactory one.

This is the time, while still working with paper and colour, to experiment with possible fabrics. As can be seen in the illustration on page 29, floral, striped, spotted and plain alter the character of the design.

'*Christ in Glory*' *patchwork altar hanging by Ade Bethune from the Church of the Sacred Heart in Vernon, Connecticut, U.S.A. Photo: Robert Pugliese.*

A skirt made from long hexagons, which are adjusted in size to fit the shape of the garment and to provide a smooth, flowing line.

Background for Box Patterns

From this stage in the instructions, ideas will be put forward to guide the worker into fresh channels of design. For instance, you may wish to space the boxes, rather than have an all–over effect as on page 25. First draw the boxes in position with the idea of putting a darker, plain colour round; from this it will be found that hex–agons and diamonds form a simple link. The interest of perspective then develops, so a plan is made for the link patches only. A step effect could be obtained with the hexagons darker than the diamonds, or vice versa.

This layout spaces the boxes rather far apart, so they are placed nearer, just touching at the points in rows. The background space divides into squares and long hexagons.

If the points of the boxes and sides touch, then diamonds fill the space.

When the distances between the boxes are equal, then the linking shapes are squares and octagons.

These examples show some of the various effects which can be explored before commencing the actual stitch–ing.

Note that some patterns work out more clearly if a larger scale is used on the isometric paper.

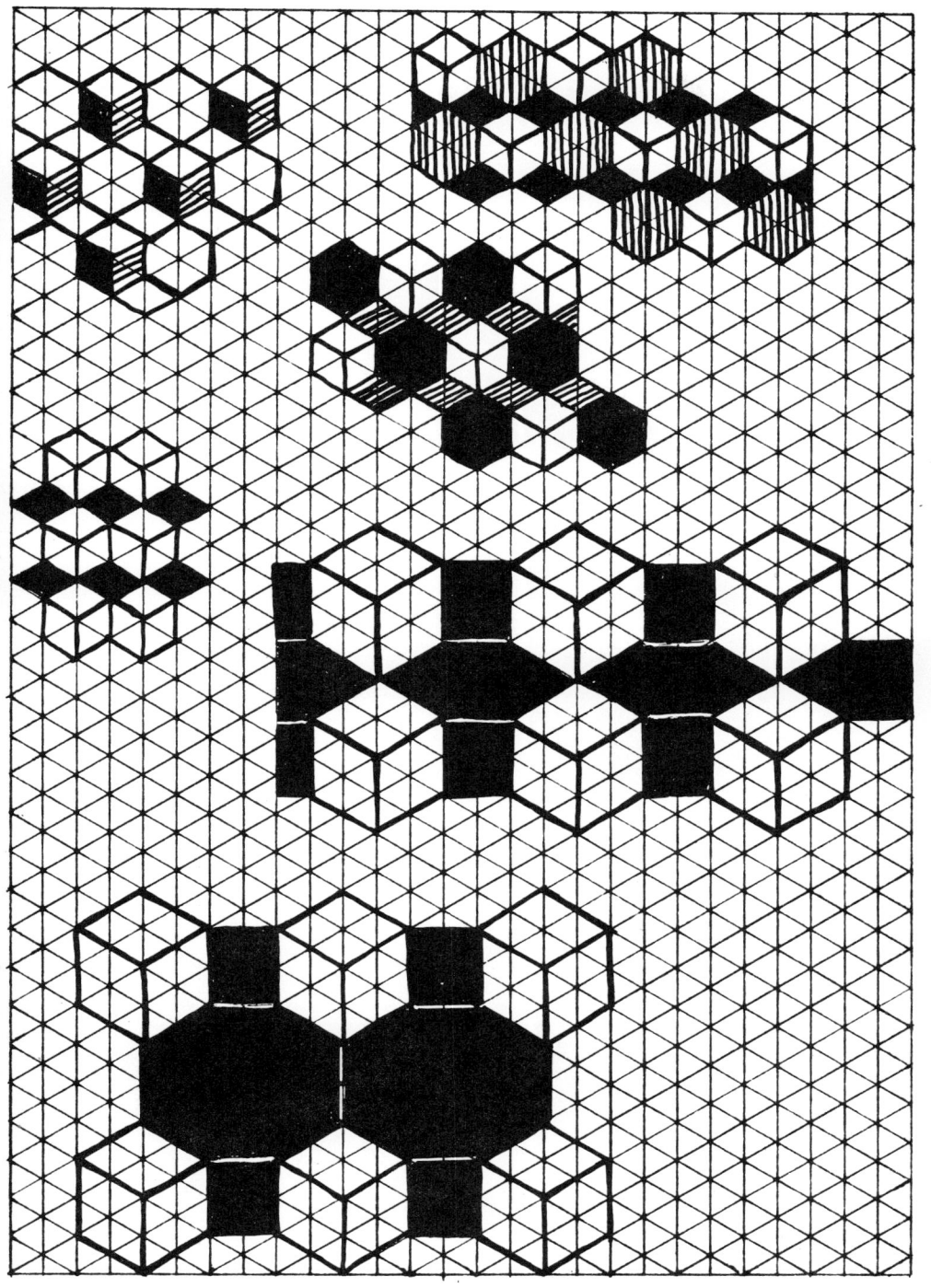

31

Combining Two Shapes

A simple example is hexagons and diamonds. First make a conventional rosette motif as described on page 16, then fill in at the edges with fitting diamonds. This will alter the motif to a large hexagon.

The illustration opposite shows how the same patterned and plain materials can be arranged to give two entirely different effects. The patterned material is a Mexican print.

These particular examples were made into table mats by using heavy Vilene as the template for the plain lining. The lining is cut to the full size of the mat, then tacked in position and oversewn to the outside edge of the motif. Although the stitches show, careful, even stitching in matching thread can look quite neat and the general finish is more tailored than trying to turn it inside out, or slip stitching on the right side.

Vilene is the trade name for a non–woven fabric made in various grades and is generally used for interlinings (see page 84).

Two arrangements of the same materials, using hexagons and diamonds

Pattern and Plain

This next exercise is based on taking one patterned fabric and two linking, plain–coloured ones, or shades of one colour.

Consider the possible use of hexagons, diamonds and stripes. To avoid confusion, first plan one shape, such as the large hexagon in patterned fabric, then sketch various colour or tonal arrangements of the supporting shapes.

As long as only plain colours are used, the size of the template is just the personal taste of the worker, but once patterned material is used, the size must be in relation to the pattern. Sometimes the exact template size is not readily available, so a simple solution is to cut the paper templates from the isometric paper. This not only ensures accurate cutting, but if the whole layout of the pattern is drafted to size, each shape will be ready to use, and it is also much easier to calculate the amount of fabric required.

Adapting Shapes to Fit a Patterned Fabric

While every pattern could lead to many varieties of shapes, just one has been used here to explain the method.

In the specimen of the material it will be seen that there is an area of plain material between the small sprigs, and this was used to develop an individual shape. First the sprig was measured on to isometric paper and set in the centre of a hexagon; then two sides of the hexagon were extended to a point as far as the plain colour would allow.

Various patterns can be developed from this shape. In the one illustrated, the patches are arranged so that the long points fit into each other, thus giving two rows of sprigs with plain material in between. To complete this particular plan, two rows of hexagons are added, using the two shades in the colour of the sprigs.

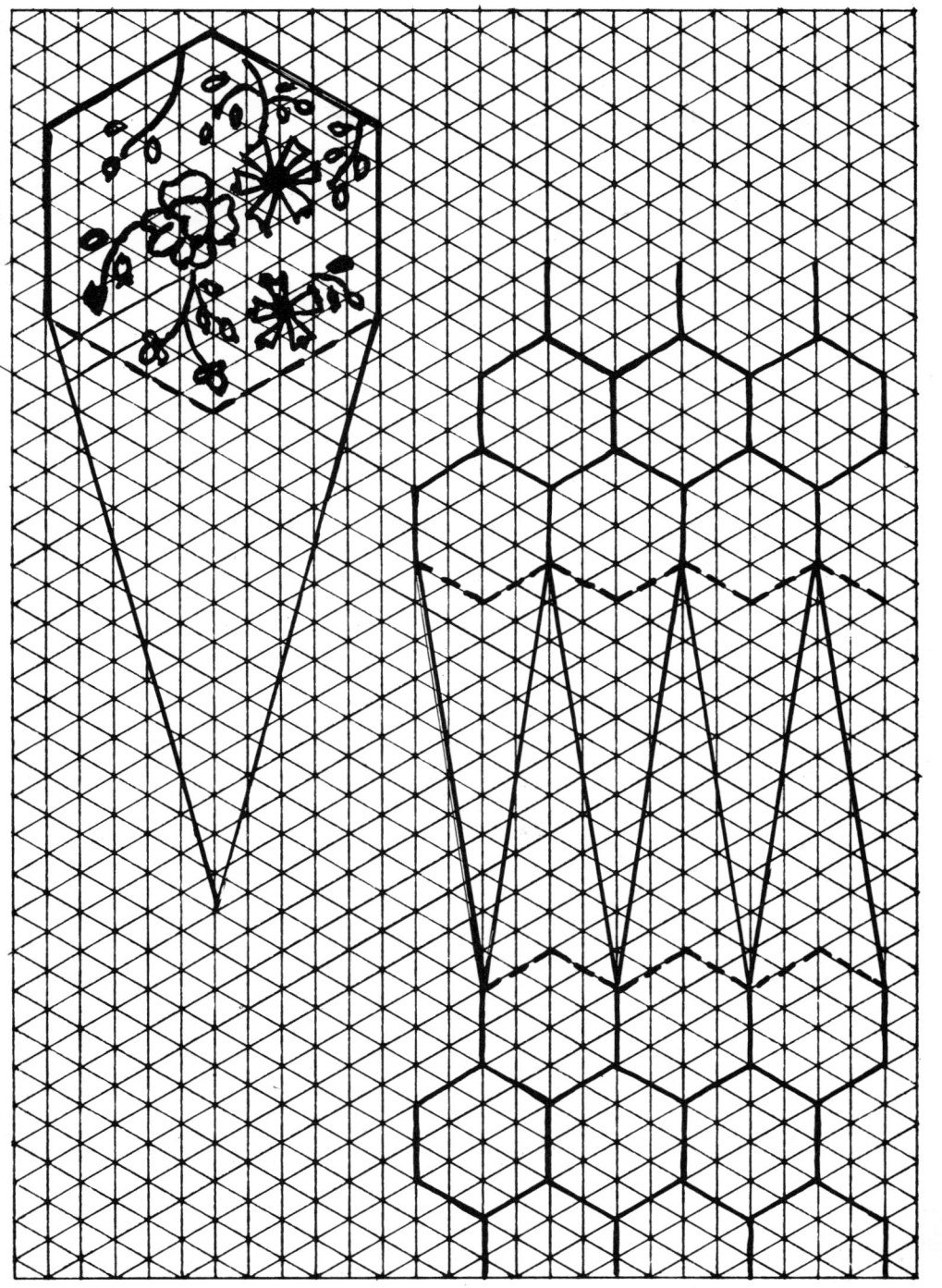

37

Adapting shapes to fit a patterned fabric

Two Different Effects from the Same Fabric

The printed cotton chosen for this exercise has wide stripes made up of a row of small flowers, with a scalloped border each side. The background is green and the stripes mainly red. This fabric was made in France, but is typical of a mid–European peasant style. The plain colour is matching red poplin.

The illustrations for the first arrangement are on pages 40 and 41; those for the second arrangement are on pages 42 and 43.

The first arrangement was planned as follows. Measure one small flower as the centre hexagon and draw this to size on isometric paper.

Draw a narrow border round, to be in a plain colour.

From the points of the hexagon radiate lines until two are far enough apart to match the width of the full stripe of the material.

The lines are then drawn parallel to form a stripe, extending the length to suit a cushion or any other suitable article, and adjusting the exact length to fit the printed pattern. The spaces between the stripes are in plain colour.

The outline can be arranged as a hexagon or as a twelve–sided figure.

To give a framed effect and to provide an interesting variation, use only the flowers and the one scalloped edge of the bands for the stripes round the edge.

The second arrangement began with a larger central hexagon, and stripes of pattern and plain were developed parallel to the sides of the hexagon. As it would confuse the effect if the printed stripes varied in width, the plain bands were drafted wider near the centre and narrower towards the edge.

From these two examples it can be seen that every striped fabric can provide an entirely individualistic effect.

The whole patterns were drafted on isometric paper, then the various shapes cut out to be used as templates. If the sheets of isometric paper are not large enough, cut the plain white border off one sheet and stick into place overlapping the white border of another sheet, matching the lines exactly.

The first arrangement of a pattern from a printed fabric

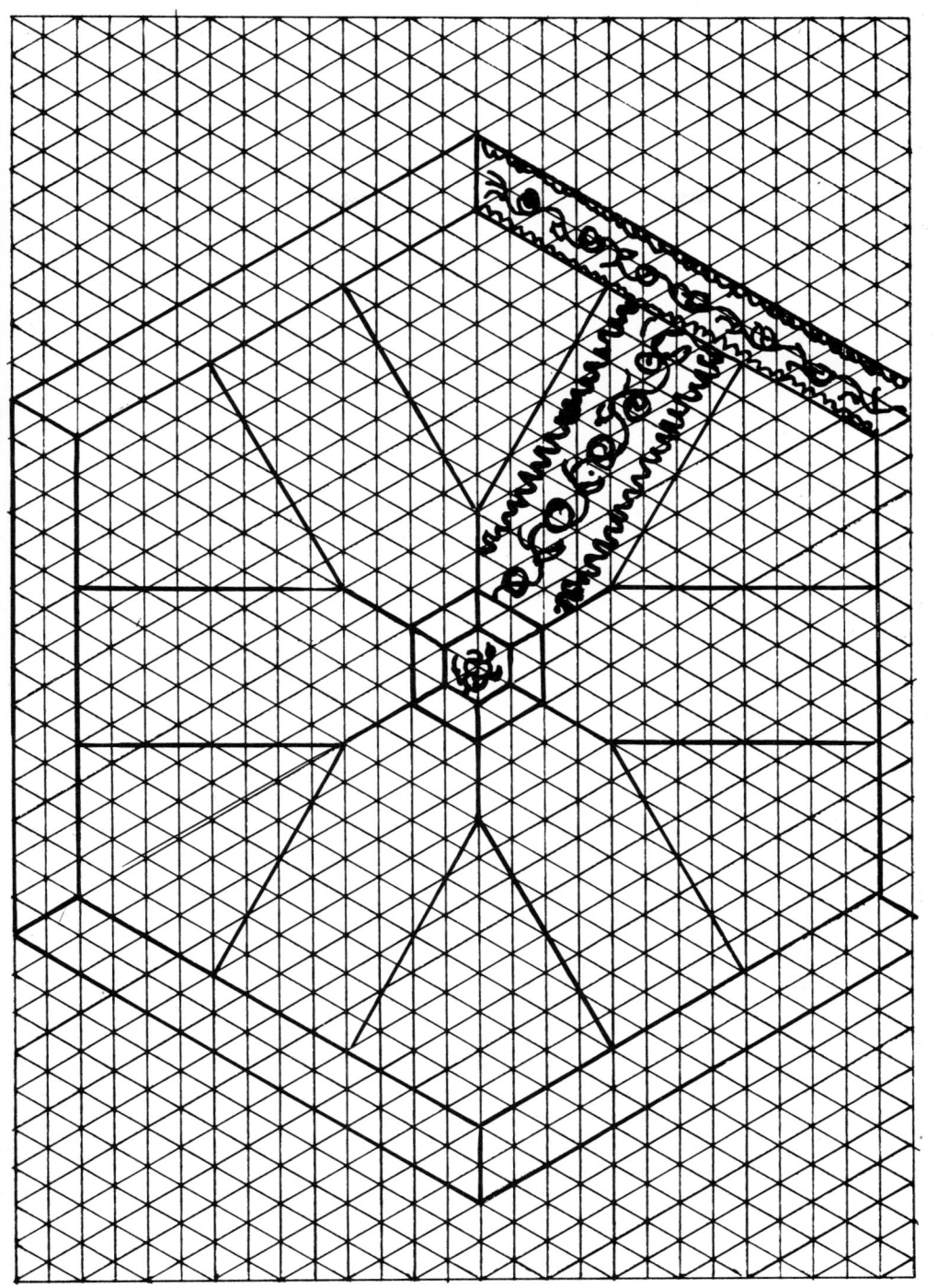

The second arrangement of a pattern from a printed fabric

Squares

Squares can give an entirely different effect from any other patchwork shape, but it is essential that the measurement, handling and stitching of each patch is absolutely accurate. For this reason all the patches in one article should be made from materials of the same weight.

The design is planned on squared paper. Commence by exploring the ways a square can be divided, shading in parts (see page 45).

Next cut out 2″ squares; then with a contrasting paper, preferably gum–backed, cut the shaded shapes and stick in place in the whole square. Make a selection of all these, and on a flat surface move them around to form various patterns.

The interpretation into materials can be entirely geometric, or small, all–over patterns are sometimes effective. However, do not lose the character of the design. The size of the squares used can be large, such as 4″ or 5″. In fact, small squares tend to look bulky due to the many seams.

Panel using plastics in various textures.

A satin box showing the imaginative use of a woven fabric motif.

The lid of a hexagonal box showing the relationships of different fabrics to patchwork shapes.

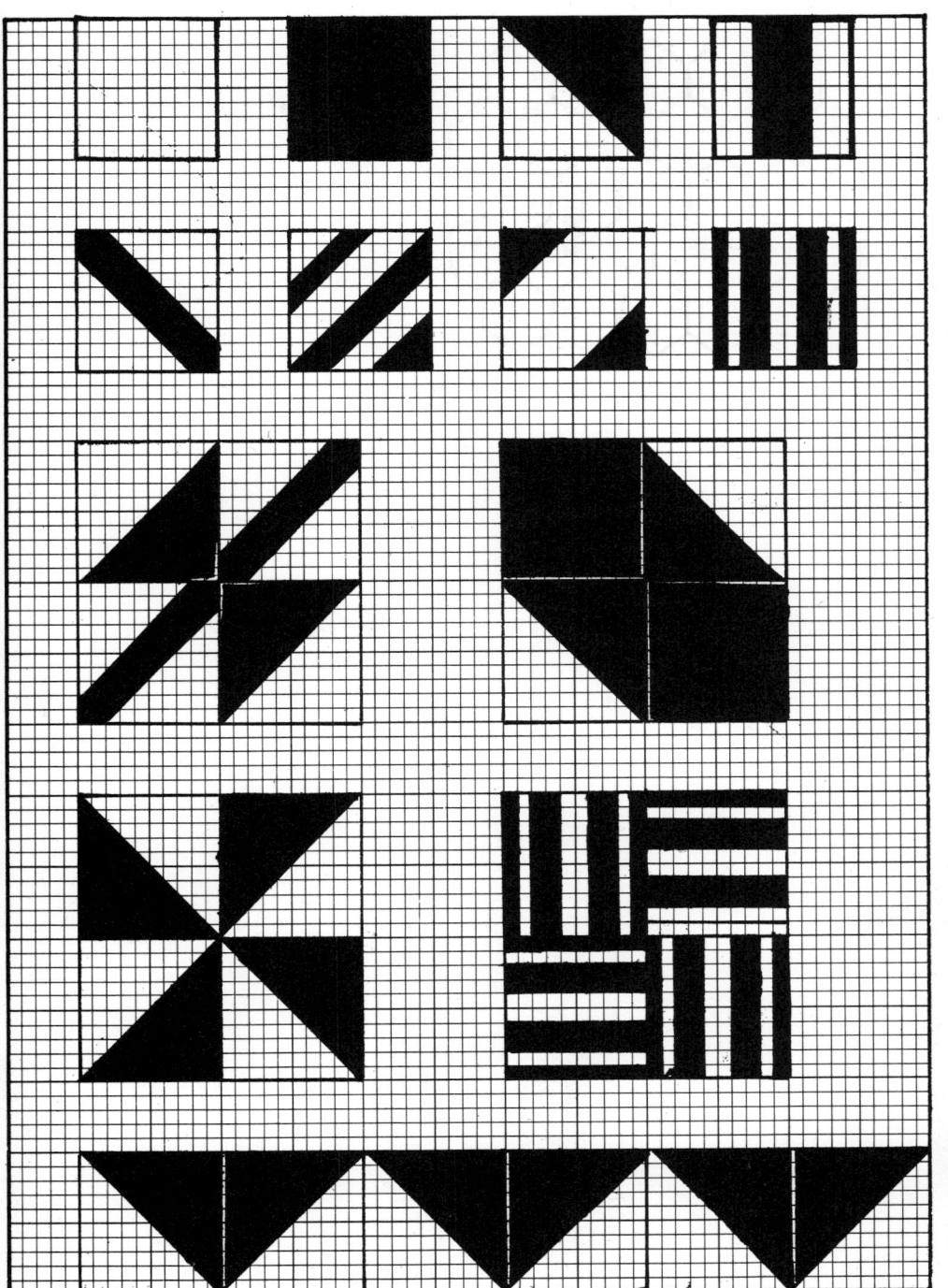

45

Perspective and Borders

Squares can be arranged to give interesting perspective, and in the interpretation of it take into account the colour effects. A light colour will appear nearer and the darkest further away, while pattern, or perhaps texture, will often complement the other two, adding a special dimension. Sometimes when two shapes are put side by side the joining line can be omitted, thus giving a variation of shape. This can be seen on the two squares illustrated, where the joining shape has been shaded.

Borders are often necessary to complete a piece of patchwork, but must be in character with the main design. It is therefore necessary to find just the right one by experimenting first on paper.

A side panel from the Sherborne Triptych in the Almshouse of SS John. (By kind permission of The Master and Brethren of the Almshouse of St John the Baptist and St John the Evangelist, Sherborne, Dorset)

Division of Squares

A design for an extra large cushion, 33″ square, was inspired by a tiled floor. Various old tiled floors were considered, but when a fifteenth-century painted triptych was seen in the Chapel of the Almshouse of SS John at Sherborne, Dorset, England, the patterned floor on one panel was sketched and found to be of a very simple construction (see the photograph on page 48). It is based on plain squares and squares divided in half diagonally, with a linking square divided into four triangles.

Light blue and dark blue poplin were chosen for the cushion and the squares used are 3″. The templates were cut from squared paper.

A pillow and a small eiderdown were put into this cushion without over-stuffing it, which suggests an idea for those who live in bed–sitting rooms. One side of the cushion would of course be left unseamed and closed with a zip or other suitable fastener.

An outsize cushion

Patchwork as a Background for Embroidery

This is not a method that suits every type of embroidery, but occasionally the worker finds it necessary to make the background as part of the design. Patchwork has the advantage over appliqué that the seams do not require neatening on the right side.

Points to consider:

Almost any straight-sided shapes can be fitted together, although inverted points, where it would be necessary to snip the turnings, would cause a weakness when joining the patches. This shape can still be included if a straight line is drawn from the point to the opposite side of the shape, thus making two patches. If necessary these two patches can still be the same colour, but the extra strength is worth the work.

If silks or fine lawns are being used, the templates can be cut in calico, and the tacking stitches holding just the turnings and calico, not through to the right side, are left in.

Sometimes the completed background, when papers are removed, is not firm enough to hold the embroidery stitches. The most satisfactory way is to put calico or linen on a square embroidery frame, then mount the patchwork, remembering to keep both slack until the edges of the patchwork are stitched down. Then tighten the frame ready for the embroidery.

One special point to remember is to allow larger turnings on the outside edges of the patchwork to facilitate making up or mounting with a frame.

Part of a panel worked by Muriel Root. The foundation consists of 2" squares of silks and fine cottons in shades of pink, red, orange and purple. The whole is covered with net to soften the overall effect by toning the colours and merging the hard, joining lines of the patchwork. Two areas of embroidery worked on top of the net are shown in this illustration. These conform to the character of the squares, yet by allowing the beads and sequins to spray, there is an added interest. (Photograph: Alan Watts)

Boxes Based on the Patchwork Principle

This pattern can be drafted to any required size and the triangles form‑ing the lid can be made longer to give a higher shape.

Cut each piece of pattern in firm card. The choice of card is decided by the size of the box. It should always be firm, yet a very small box would be bulky made with the heavy card needed for a large size. The worker must try out a selection of cards, perhaps using various household packages as a guide. These can be made into the finished box pro‑viding colour and print do not show through the materials.

Cut cards with a Stanley knife, cut‑ting against a steel rule. Cut the material, allowing turnings of not less than $\frac{3}{8}''$. The turnings are held in place over each piece of card with a light adhesive. Leave the points free as these can be adjusted when stitching.

First sew the four sides to the square base, right sides facing, as for patch‑work.

Next join the sides together by over‑sewing on the right side. Join the four lid pieces to the tops of the sides but not to each other.

The satin lining is made up using either thin card or Vilene templates. It is necessary to cut the templates a fraction smaller than the pattern.

Join the lining pieces in the same order as the box and place neatly into the box.

Finally, oversew the edges of the lining to the four lid sections. Slip stitch can be used, but neat over‑sewing is in character with the rest of the stitching.

The fastening of the lid can be a hand‑made cord threaded through buttonhole loops at each point. Finish the cord ends with a tassel, or a knob made by detached buttonhole stitch. The cord should be long enough to allow the box to open fully—try it with string first.

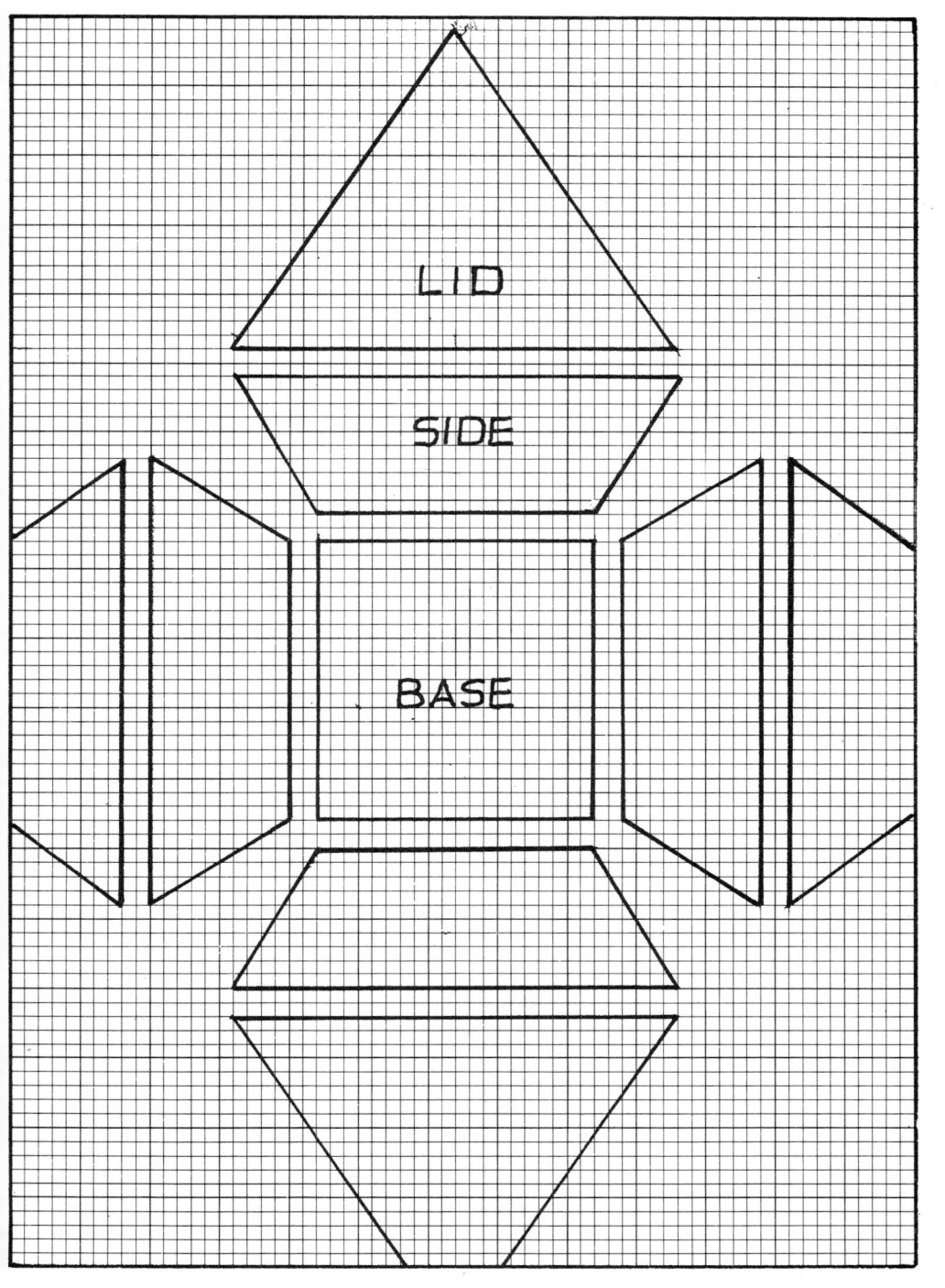

LID

SIDE

BASE

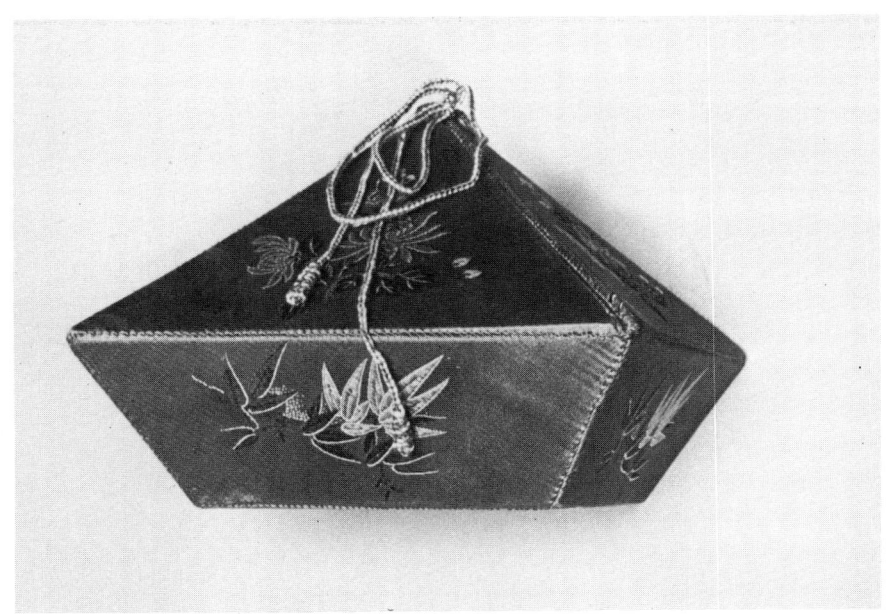

A blue satin box. Note that the sprigs of the design are chosen to fit the particular shape of each patch. Designed by Margaret Taylor. (Photograph: Paul Meidman)

A Box for the Bathroom

This box is made from the same pattern as on page 55, but being on a larger scale, made in towelling and lined with light–weight plastic cloth, it can be used in the bathroom for toiletries. The base is 7″ square, the sides are 3½″ deep and the triangle lid from base to point is 7″.

The outside shapes are covered with printed towelling. Embroidery can be used to accentuate the design. In this particular pattern the central circles are embroidered in black wool. The stitches must be simple, such as twisted chain and french knots, because the loops of the towelling tend to pull through with the wool.

The thin lining card is cut out as one large pattern with the lid sections ¼″ smaller. The position of the folds can be lightly scored. To cover with the plastic, stick the turnings and points in place, but leave the sides of the box part free. Put the lining into the box and neaten the sides by arranging the turnings so that one folds back on to its own card and the other fits behind, thus avoiding any gaps. Carefully stick in position. Adhesive applied on the point of a

A towelling box made for the bathroom (shown closed). (Photograph: Paul Meidman)

tapestry needle will neaten the corners.

The lid sections are slip–stitched on to the towelling rather than over–sewed, which might tear the plastic.

Triangular tabs backed with Velcro (see page 84) are stitched at the points and these, when pinched to–gether, give a neat handy fastening to the lid.

Towelling box (*shown open*). (*Photograph: Paul Meidman*)

Hexagonal Box

This box is made from a 4½″, equilateral hexagonal base, and the sides are 2½″ deep. The lid is a 5″ equilateral hexagon. The design on the lid is made first from seven hexagons (1½″) in shades of blue silk with diamonds of checked silk to complete the main hexagon shape of the box. Smaller hexagonal patches (¾″) of the checked silk are made using medium Vilene for the templates. They are applied by slip stitch to the top of the basic patches. The narrow silver braid and threads are arranged to develop the design.

The sides of the box are made as patches using heavy Vilene for the templates. This gives the silk a lightly padded quality, which improves the general finish. The whole box is stiffened with card inside and the lining is lightly padded with Courtelle wadding.

This idea should not be copied exactly, but rather used as an example of material and colours dictating the final effect.

Hexagonal box built up of hexagons, diamonds and rectangles. (*Photograph: Paul Meidman*)

Patchwork as an Exercise in Design

The use of fabrics to learn more about design will often help a worker who finds the paper, pencil and paint method uninspiring.

A furnishing fabric that has a large, simple motif is a good beginning. Cut the motif as a square or rectangle, then cut it into four strips of varying widths. Cut matching paper templates $\frac{1}{4}''$ smaller all round, and tack the strips on to the paper.

Now lay these strips on to a sheet of white paper and retaining the basic design, move them to show white between. When a satisfactory arrangement has been achieved, mark and cut the white strips of background paper, cover with white material and join all the strips together.

The paper could be in a dark colour and other variations explored, such as arranging in steps the sections of the basic design.

Cutting a printed motif into sections. (Photograph: Paul Meidman)

61

A Pentagon and Striped Material

To experiment with a striped mater–
ial, an irregular pentagon (five–sided
shape) is drawn in the centre of a
square. Lines are arranged, one from
each point of the pentagon, to the
sides of the square. The pentagon
can be one colour or, as in the
example, divided into five unequal
triangles in order to use the plain
coloured stripes of the material to
accentuate the centre.

The outside shapes are covered with
the striped material, varying the
angles of the stripes, and the patches
are then joined together.

This may not be an exciting design
but the planning can be used to
learn more of the possibilities of
stripes and straight lines.

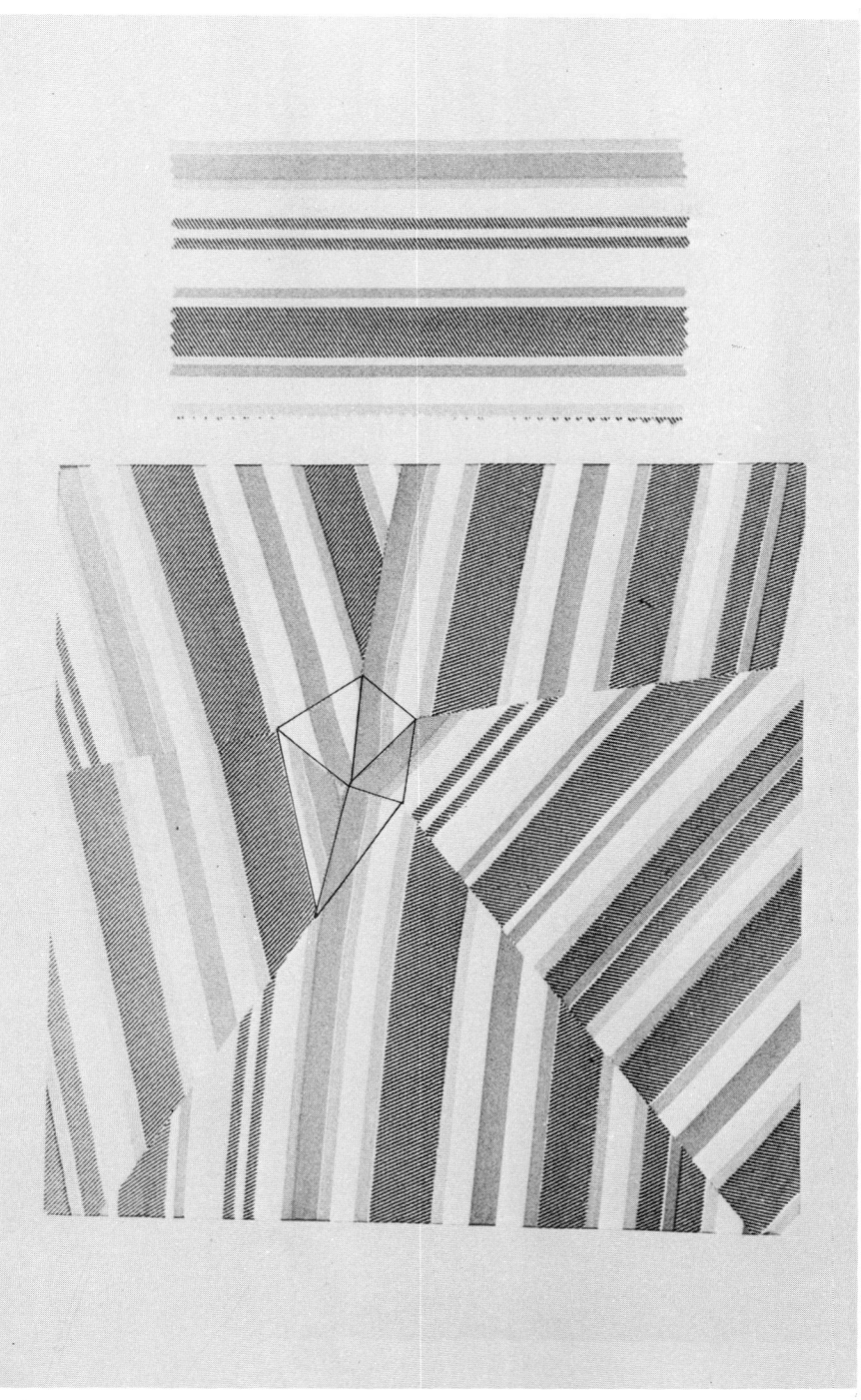

The development of an irregular pentagon. (Photograph: Paul Meidman)

The Development of a New Idea

The next three lessons give detailed explanations of how an idea, apparently remote from patchwork, developed step by step into practical patchwork. It is not intended that this idea should be copied exactly, but rather to encourage the search for fresh study.

The leaves of the *Monstera deliciosa* plant are fascinating with their holes and the curved edges of each division making a large curved leaf.

FIRST STAGE

First the outlines were sketched, then the holes and background shaded in. The desire was to interpret directly into patchwork, using a bright green Hawaiian cotton printed in a blurred all–over design, and a dark green of the same pattern. These materials convey' the effect of the leaves growing on the sidewalks in Hawaii with the sun shining.

Manipulation of all the small intricate shapes would have been too difficult in paper, so the design was drawn on calico and cut out to use as templates.

While this design could have been completed by much careful work it was not entirely satisfactory, particularly where the narrow turnings had to be snipped to make them flat, thus causing a weakness.

Finally, the conclusion was that appliqué would be a better and more accurate technique in the interpretation of this particular design.

Showing the various stages of an idea. (Photograph: Paul Meidman)

SECOND STAGE

The curves at the edges of the leaves, with the section narrowing towards the main vein, still seemed interesting. This shape was simplified to a long triangle, curving the short end in towards the point.

As can be seen from the illustration, the triangles fit into each other, bringing out the feature of the curve and returning once again to holes.

The triangle measurements are $8\frac{1}{2}''$ × $5\frac{3}{4}''$, with a $\frac{3}{4}''$ deep curve.

To accentuate the shapes it was decided to make them alternate light and dark blue, using a fairly heavy satin, with the templates in medium Vilene.

While realising that the curve is not pure patchwork, to achieve the desired effect it seemed practical to herringbone the turnings of the curve on to the Vilene. The rest of the joining was done by the usual over-sewing method, including the joining of the six points.

The backing, in cream satin of the same weight, was chosen to show through the holes and make a complete scheme. It seemed necessary to attach the points of the patchwork to the cream satin, so to add a soft quality a layer of medium thickness Terylene wadding was put behind the whole patchwork and the points stitched right through as invisibly as possible.

A geometric development of a section of the leaf. (Photograph: Paul Meidman)

THIRD STAGE

A further idea of unattached patches led to the plan of making squares in gingham with a metal eyelet in each corner, through which narrow white tape could be threaded to link the corners of four patches.

The following steps to find the right scale and thickness are included to illustrate the need to search for exactly the best result.

First three different pattern sizes of gingham were bought in dark brown and the same sizes in plum red to make a reversible cover for a bunk bed.

The largest squared gingham set the size when a dark square of the check—ed pattern was planned in each corner of the patch. This led to deciding on $4\frac{1}{2}''$ square as a workable size for each patch.

Next Vilene, instead of paper, as a template was tried out, but the result did not give sufficient support to the eyelets. A $\frac{1}{4}''$ thick foam was put between the two gingham squares, but this was not entirely satisfactory as the turnings sometimes showed through to the right side, and anyway only one square could be tacked on to the foam while the other was difficult to manipulate. Finally, $\frac{1}{8}''$ thick foam was used as a template for both squares, which were then oversewn together on the right side. This ensured sharp neat corners in character with the gingham. Brass eyelets, $\frac{3}{16}''$ in diameter, were inserted at each corner about $\frac{1}{2}''$ from the edge.

There could have been many variations to the over–all plan of the squares, but the one chosen was brown on one side with the plum red on the other. The illustration shows the diagonal layout.

The narrow tape was cut into $18''$ lengths and threaded through the four eyelets to give a square effect one side and a cross on the other, with the ends tied into a neat firm bow. The edge pairs of eyelets were also tied together.

Gingham squares forming a cover for a bunk bed. (Photograph: Paul Meidman)

Unusual Materials

Patchwork for practical use, such as domestic and clothing, must use reliable materials—those which give accurate folding, equal wearing qualities and are suitable for washing or dry–cleaning. But for purely decorative patchwork in the wall panel category, the scope for experimenting is endless.

The panel illustrated is made from plastics in varying gold textures using the clamshell template. This shape, although in the patchwork list, is more an appliqué method. The shape is usually cut with turnings and only the top curve is tacked over the template, usually of Vilene, then each row of curves covers the edges of the previous row of 'stems'. They are stitched by fine hemming, on the right side, on to a backing. When using the plastic, each shape was cut without turnings, as the material does not fray, to the exact size of the template and stitched or carefully stuck in position. In the centre three patches were cut as one shape to give a smooth effect. An extra decoration was added by cutting out the centres of four shapes and placing the outline shapes overlapping the solid areas.

The rich texture and beautiful colours of velvets could be used for a wall hanging or panel.

Many generations of workers have used the valuable scraps from their ragbags. The early settlers in America used woollen scraps with great care, but perhaps the most economical is a bed cover, seen in a Sussex village rectory, which made use of the least worn parts of men's flannel shirts, including sections of the collars. The shapes were fitted together at odd angles to avoid any waste. The only decorative feature was bright green wool knotted on the right side at regular intervals to hold the patchwork, interlining and backing together.

Examples of Victorian crazy patchwork covers can sometimes be seen in museums. All kinds of materials were used, and each irregular–shaped patch overlapped the raw edges of the previous patch, being tacked in place on a backing. The backing was usually sheeting or calico, but stiff paper was sometimes used. The edges of the patches were decorated with stitches, such as feather, buttonhole, chain and fly with variations. The embroidery threads economically used up the oddments from the work box, but if several skeins of gold–coloured silk were available the finished result was considered rather special. If paper backing had been used it was torn away when the embroidery stitches were completed.

Present–day jackets, waistcoats and handbags are sometimes made from scraps of leather or suede. Often they are not really attractively planned, but as articles of clothing they offer much scope for individual design.

Panel using gold plastics. (Photograph: Paul Meidman)

71

A Spanish Skirt

This skirt was made to order in Spain and consists of pieces of silk folded into approximately 1½″ equilateral triangles which are stitched on to a backing, such as fine cotton, commencing with the row at the bottom of the skirt. The raw edges and stitches are then covered by the points of the next row.

To make the triangles cut a 2″ wide bias strip and cut into 3″ lengths. Fold a ½″ turning on one long edge to the wrong side. Take the left–hand end of the turning and fold over to the right (an angle of 60°) to form a triangle with its point in the centre of the turning fold.

Lift the right–hand end over to the left on top of the triangle to make a treble thickness triangle, with all the raw edges, except the base, hidden inside. Trim the points from the base.

Stitch the raw edges into position on the backing using running stitch or back stitch, and make one invisible stitch to hold the point in place.

The illustrations showing the stages of folding are with striped material to indicate the bias, but the original skirt is made up of patterned and plain silks in bright colours and is most effective.

These petal shapes could be used in various experiments, such as a long evening skirt with much larger petals at the bottom, getting smaller towards the waist. If a larger–scale petal is used, it might be necessary to slip stitch together the open sides of the triangle. Also actual weight of the skirt will need to be taken into account, as the original short skirt weighs 18 oz, which feels quite heavy.

In the original, the waist was stitched on to a length of petersham ribbon and a fine silk lining was added.

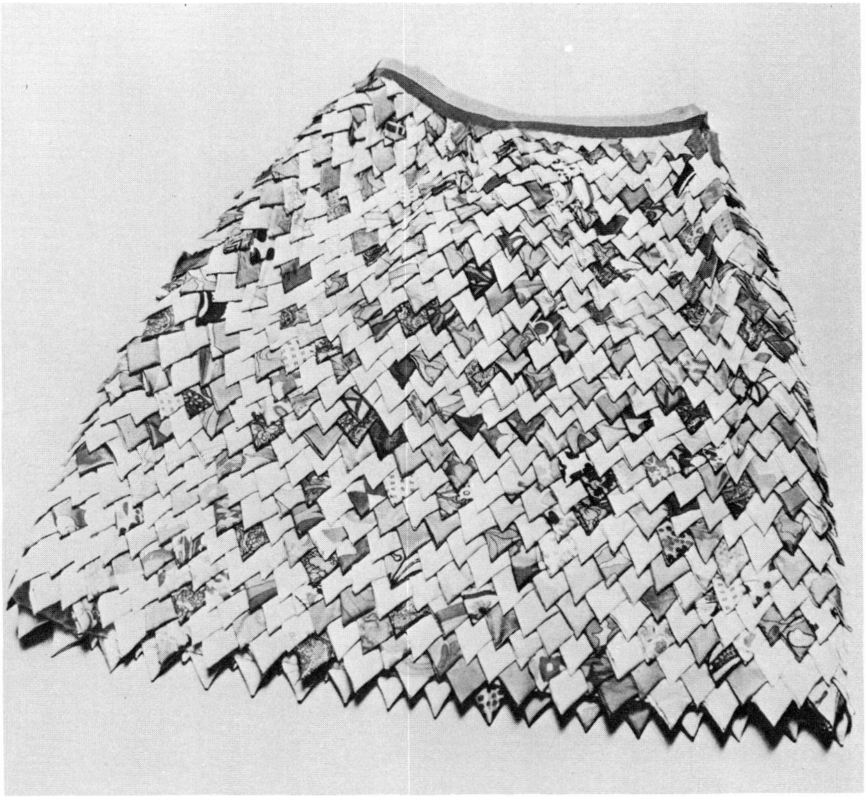

A Spanish skirt. (Photograph: Paul Meidman)

*Method of folding patches for
the Spanish skirt
(Photographs: Paul Meidman)*

Detail of an example of Seminole Indian patchwork. (Photograph: Paul Meidman)

Patchwork of the Seminole Indians

In Florida, USA, the Seminole Indians make and wear costumes which incorporate their unique style of patchwork. It is made as a strip set between bands of plain–coloured materials.

The patchwork strip, as seen in the example illustrated, can be made as follows.

Cut a length of bright blue cotton $\frac{6}{10}$" wide plus turnings. The length is as long as the fabric allows. Join to this three narrow strips $\frac{3}{10}$" wide plus turnings; first white, then orange and dark green. The joining is done by sewing–machine using white cotton throughout.

The fifth strip is pink, the same width and length as the blue, and joined on to the green.

Cut this striped patchwork into 1" pieces and rejoin to give $\frac{1}{2}$" sections, placing the colours in a stepping pattern.

Finally, the patchwork is joined, top and bottom, on to strips of plain contrasting cotton or satin and in so doing is positioned to make the blocks of patchwork slanting.

The plain bands are decorated by rows of very narrow vandyke braid in various colours.

The colour schemes vary with each article of clothing. A blouse–type shirt worn by one of the Indian men was mainly pale pink satin with very fine patchwork insets. The women wear full skirts. It is possible to obtain a similar effect, though on a larger scale, by the conventional method of patchwork.

The illustration on page 76 is enlarged to show how the pieces are cut and joined together.

Method of preparing and inserting the patchwork made by the Seminole Indians

Things to Make

Bedspread This can be a cover over the whole bed with a lining, or for warmth it can be interlined with Terylene wadding. If the bed has a valance, the cover is made smaller to just overlap it.

Pram and cot covers should be washable.

Cushions are most interesting as all shapes and sizes are practical.

Chair seat pad in character with the chair.

Bags All sizes, from small–scale patchwork for evening bags, perhaps using some of the dress material, to shoulder–strap bags for day wear. Bright beach bags lined with plastic offer great scope for experimenting with patterns and colours, which would not normally be suitable for more conventional uses.

Curtains Border patterns make an interesting trimming on plain curtains.

Knee rugs made in woollen materials and lined with a fine warm cloth.

Clothing Long and short skirts, waistcoats, even long coats can be successful additions to a wardrobe, providing the colours are selected carefully and the whole outfit is linked in a similar style. The making–up must be neat, and washing or dry–cleaning taken into account.

Wall panels should be designed for the position where they will be hung. Patchwork always, shows to advantage if surrounded by plain colour—too much pattern gives a sense of confusion.

Church vestments and furnishings are sometimes made in patchwork. They are usually very beautiful, using rich fabrics in glowing colours. The design and colour scheme must always take into account the setting in which it will be used, the lighting of the church and the predominant colour stated by the stained glass windows or the carpets.

Suggestions for Finishing and Lining

When all the patches are joined, and before removing the papers, gently press on the right side to make the article the correct shape and flat. Then remove the papers and press again, taking care not to stretch the individual patches.

Twisting or knotting threads can spoil rhythmic stitching, which is really part of the pleasure of patch–work. First thread the needle with the end coming from the reel. Secondly, do not have too long a needleful.

Patches with narrow turnings can be difficult to manipulate and it is usually much better to discard them and re-cut.

To keep templates in their correct positions on the design, mark or number them on the side visible while working, before covering with fabric. This will prevent them from being reversed.

Breaking thread can be caused by a rough eye of the needle, rough thim–ble or using a jerking movement when pulling the thread through. Often the worker is not aware of this action. It is necessary to relax and stitch with a smooth, even tension.

It is wiser to enjoy the actual stitching than rush to complete the work.

A fractional adjustment of a stripe or the way a sprig design will link with another makes all the difference in giving the appearance of skilled work.

To keep patches and templates tidy, thread a template and its matching patch on a length of cotton. Each section of the design can be threaded on one length of cotton with its own paper template in order of use. The only time this is not a suitable method is with materials likely to mark; these can be kept in small boxes.

Before cutting patches press out any creases.

If the paper templates happen to get folded before being made up, they can be pressed with a warm iron.

When holding the two patches between first finger and thumb of the left hand ready to oversew, keep the edges along the finger rather than stretched over, which alters the relative position of the patches.

Do not give two pulls to a needleful of thread—it is a waste of time. It is better to take a shorter thread.

If using a backing fabric, such as calico or Vilene, instead of paper templates, then only tack through the turning and backing so that these stitches can be left in when the work is finished and the backing will be held in place permanently.

Fraying fabrics are not easy to use, but if it is necessary for a particular effect, a simple way to deal with the problem is first to cut the patch carefully, then spray the cut edges with a colourless fixative spray, usually used in art for fixing charcoal drawings. An alternative is a hair spray without lanolin.

When using patterned materials look to see if the pattern is woven or printed. If woven it will probably be more accurate in relation to the warp and weft of the weave and in the spacing. Often a printed design is less accurate. In this case cut for the design and take more care when folding and stitching, as patches just off the straight of the thread can easily pull out of shape.

When mounting patchwork on a card, board or backing, check that all the turnings of the patches are flat in their original positions, pressing into place with the point of a warm iron. If the mount is hard, cover with a layer of the thinnest Courtelle wadding, or very thin plastic foam. The turnings will settle into the pad and not show from the right side.

Using materials already in hand, or buying new ones often causes discussion. A safe rule is to use as many as possible from the rag bag, but only if they really fit the scheme. Often it is necessary to buy extra plain colours and the linking material to join motifs, as in the bedspread on page 18.

It is wise to note that cotton materials are a seasonal stock in many shops and the next year will bring different dyes.

Small local shops will often stock different materials from the stores.

EDGES

A fine piping cord covered with a bias strip of the matching materials is the neatest edge to patchwork, giving a straight line. The cord should be shrunk before covering. The piping is set where all the patches are even and the shaped edges trimmed after. The lining or backing is slip-stitched on the reverse side against the piping. It is often easier to curve corners than to make a sharp point.

Another way is to mount the edge

row of patches on to a backing or lining. First, with the lining turn and tack a deep hem, such as 4″, omitting the small turning. Mitre the corners neatly. Next lay the edge row of the patches in position, allowing 2″ or 3″ of the lining to show. Tack in place, then hem round the edge of the patches, taking the stitches through the two layers of lining. The colour of the lining would of course belong to the scheme of the patchwork.

If a serrated effect is in keeping with the article, the edge row of patches can be backed by another set of ′ patches, oversewing the outside edges. Then the lining can be slip–stitched in position on to the back patches, making it invisible from the right side.

very small back stitches through to the patchwork side, then tie the ends of the thread into an ordinary knot on the lining side. Cut the ends of the thread long enough to be firm during wear. Sometimes these knots are spaced to form a pattern on the patchwork side.

LINING

The lining of an article, such as a bedspread, must be attached to the patchwork to keep the finished work smooth during use. There are two methods. One is to tack the turnings of the lining joins to the turnings of the patches, then the edges are slip–stitched into place.

The alternative is to make up the whole bedspread and lay it out flat on the floor or a large table, lining side up. At regular intervals make two

Patchwork to See

In all parts of the world, patchwork has been made and found its way into museums and collections which are available to the public for study. There are also examples of present-day work being used in churches (see the colour photograph facing page 28). Obviously it is not possible to provide a comprehensive list, but some of the lesser-known patchwork is included here. It is worthwhile finding out if any examples of patchwork can be seen in the area where you live, or are visiting. It is suggested that you find out the times of opening to avoid disappointment.

ENGLAND

There are several museums that specialise in patchwork quilts, and in England the finest display is at the American Museum in Britain, Claverton Manor, Bath, Avon.

The Embroiderers' Guild, 73 Wimpole Street, London, has some beautiful examples of patchwork in its collection. Visitors are requested, if possible, to make an appointment to see any special type of work.

The textile museum of London is the Victoria and Albert Museum, South Kensington, where work which is not on exhibition can, by special arrangement, be made available for study in the Students' Room.

Small local museums often have one particularly interesting example and it is worth even a short visit. For example, the museum at Worthing in West Sussex has a good example of Victorian crazy patchwork.

Bamburgh Castle, Northumberland, has a door curtain hanging in the passageway between the Faire Chamber and the Armoury, which was made by Russian prisoners from their uniforms during the Crimean War.

King's Lynn Museum and Art Gallery, Market Street, King's Lynn, Norfolk, possesses a patchwork dressing-gown made by the school-children of Hillington, near King's Lynn, for Sir William ffoulkes on the occasion of his marriage in 1818.

SCOTLAND

The Royal Scottish Museum, Chambers Street, Edinburgh 1, has several patchwork quilts in its collection, but not always on view, including one dating from about 1825, which was acquired from the Needlework Development Scheme (Accession no. 1962/1073).

One of the most recent modern examples of patchwork is in Glasgow Cathedral. It was designed by Malcolm Lochead, DA, and worked by the members of the Glasgow branch of the Embroiderers' Guild. It is a cover for the Shrine of St Mungo.

Another example is the frontal for the communion table at Mayfield Church of Scotland, Edinburgh 9, designed and made by Kathleen Whyte. It can be seen on application to the Minister or Church Officer.

USA

The Shelburne Museum in Shelburne, Vermont, specialises in all types of bed coverings, including patchwork.

BERMUDA

The museum at St George's possesses a fine example of Victorian silk patchwork.

For Further Reading

Many books have been written dealing with various aspects of patchwork and those mentioned here are intended as a guide to the student, but it is not a comprehensive list.

Colby, Averil *Patchwork* (Batsford); a study of the history and technical methods.

Finley, Ruth E. *Old Patchwork Quilts and the Women who Made Them* (Bell); tells an interesting story of the human side of patchwork.

Green, Sylvia *Patchwork for Beginners* (Studio Vista); has many good contemporary ideas, including patch–work toys.

Ickis, Marguerite *The Standard Book of Quilt–Making and Collecting* (Dover); includes patterns and quilting based on the American styles.

Marston, Doris E. *Patchwork Today: A Practical Introduction* (Bell).

List of Suppliers

As patchwork templates are not yet sold in metric units, no metric equivalents have been used in the text of this book. However, the following list of useful metric equivalents might be found helpful.

$\frac{1}{4}$ inch = 0·6 centimetre
$\frac{1}{2}$ inch = 1·3 centimetres
$\frac{3}{4}$ inch = 2 centimetres
1 inch = 2·5 centimetres
2 inches = 5 centimetres

Metal templates and plastic window templates of various shapes and sizes can be bought at embroidery and handicraft shops. A full range is obtainable from the following:

Mace & Nairn, 89 Crane Street, Salisbury, Wiltshire SP1 2PY. If requesting material to be sent by post, send a stamped, addressed envelope for their price list.

The Needlewoman Shop, 146–148 Regent Street, London W1R 6BA. If requesting material to be sent by post, first find out what the minimum order requirement is.

Isometric paper is sold by stationers and drawing office suppliers, either as single sheets or in blocks. If you are unable to obtain this paper locally, the manufacturers, H.W. Peel & Co. Ltd, Chartwell House, Jeymer Drive, Greenford UB6 8NX, will supply a list of stockists of their Chartwell isometric pads.

Vilene is stocked by most department stores. If there is any difficulty in obtaining just the right grade, write to:

Vilene Information Service, Bondina Vilene Ltd, Greetland, Halifax, West Yorkshire.

Velcro is the trade name for a fastening made from two Nylon strips; one with tiny loops and the other with hooks. When pressed together the hooks grip the loops to give a tight secure closure. To open just peel the two strips apart. Velcro can be purchased by the yard and is stocked by most department stores. If you experience any difficulty, write to the manufacturers, Selectus Ltd, Biddulph, Stoke–on–Trent ST8 7RH.

some other Mills and Boon needlecraft books

A World of Embroidery
Mary Gostelow

Mary Gostelow has travelled widely in Europe, the Middle East, Russia and parts of Africa. She is a member of the Embroiderers' Guild, and has a personal collection of embroideries.

This richly illustrated and highly readable book is concerned with the embroidery of many nations in many eras. The techniques used to make the different stitches are carefully described and the text and line drawings skilfully combine to clarify each step. Anyone who is interested in embroidery should find this a fascinating, informative study, as well as a beautiful possession.

ISBN 0 263 05655 4

Modelling in Hessian
Margaret Hutchings

Margaret Hutchings is the author of many craft books which are popular with children and adults alike.

Modelling in Hessian should appeal to all those who enjoy sewing and experimenting with shapes. The small, timeless, faceless figures are made out of natural fabric and can be modelled into sensitive and supple forms. Precise instructions show how to make the basic figures, and photographs of the author's own experiments encourage readers to formulate their own ideas, once they have grasped the fundamental techniques.

ISBN 0 263 05693 7

Easy Embroidery
Lis Paludan

A colourful and exciting look at embroidery for young and old alike. All the basic stitches are described and illustrated. The book is packed with pictures of the author's designs, with easy to follow instructions, diagrams and same size patterns. 'Many of the designs . . . have a naive charm and freshness, and the book as a whole is a real delight to look at.'
Times Educational Supplement
ISBN 0 263 05428 4

English Embroidery
Barbara Snook

A valuable survey of English embroidery from medieval times to the present day. The author describes the changing methods of embroidery as well as the important influences from the Continent and the East. This book has been reissued, with the addition of colour and black and white photographs, in response to continuing demand.
ISBN 0 263 05579 5

Fashion Sewing for Everyone
Adele P. Margolis

A really comprehensive sewing manual which offers basic instruction for beginners and expert guidance for the more experienced. There are ideas and designs for a whole wardrobe of clothes plus valuable information on the use of difficult fabrics.
ISBN 0 263 05431 4

Crochet Pretty and Practical
Caroline Horne

Full instructions for making a variety of garments and useful small articles for the home, starting with a section on how to crochet and culminating in instructions for crocheting a wedding dress.
ISBN 0 263 05151 X

Presents and Playthings
Jean Greenhowe

The colourful items to make in this book include soft toys, dolls, glove puppets, models, miniatures and even a board game. Most of these can be made from scraps of fabrics, trimmings and household odds and ends. All the patterns are the same size and while some of the items are machine or hand sewn, others need only adhesive for their construction.
ISBN 0 263 05541 8